Tommy Archuleta

FIELDNOTES

LILY POETRY REVIEW BOOKS

Copyright © 2023 by Tommy Archuleta
Published by Lily Poetry Review Books
223 Winter Street
Whitman, MA 02382

https://lilypoetryreview.blog/

ISBN: 978-1-957755-13-7

Cover photograph: Aldous Register, "Virga"

For Diana, Claire, and Chris

FIELDNOTES

I

Breadcrumbs here
and there but not one footprint

∞

Seeing in the dark   the first

trick we learn over
those short months

in the womb
only to relearn it out here

Day in day out

∞

You there keeping track of all you've
failed to do

Why not try sleeping outside more often
roaming end

to end the entire sky
the whole night through

If doing so doesn't forgive you
then by all means

go back inside
and resume counting

II

Too difficult to tell if those crows
are joking or serious

Dangerously caffeinated or talking in their sleep

∞

How can the ghost of the orchard always
be only one moment away from bountiful

The horses out front harnessed always to carts
made of paper rather than hickory

∞

From the sound of it father has just enough
breath in him to weigh the day's gifts against his one trespass

You can't miss it

It's the one spelled out in white smoke over
the southend of town legible as any other sign out there

That is until you touch it

III

No matter the weather or
time of day
the griefstricken are too many
                       too many to count

Those cleared for flight
and the earthbound

          ∞

               Withdraw   step
by step   yes

But to what

and away from which body   the one
halfstarved always

Or the one seldom free
from the tangle of words

as Saint Ambrose would say

IV

Some nights her name
comes bounding down the canyon

the music rooting you
stories deep

Other nights
my stillborn twin hastens to

sing when frightened
and if we're ever freed   I pray at least

one of us dissolves over the sheriff's
prized cherry trees

only to recompose soon
after the two of us thereby totaling

seven   the half here
half there number

V

As for the well somewhere inside
every good father
the one assigned to hold his missteps

and those of his ancestors
and offspring both   I worry

the one inside mine is nearing full

∞

Yellowthroat   the angel of death
likes to call him
(I can see why)

Nightingale whenever he's out
drawing up song
from silence

Hardcider from darkness

Life from mostly
stonestill bodies

∞

Maybe it's best that we the lifelong
earthbound see only
one of the moon's two vying faces night
    in night out

That dreaming and forgetting are boons for
poetry teachers and ghosts alike

That one's last hour alive
is glimpsed in those seconds prior to birth

VI

In the way father invites
your ghost

out to the
garden after supper the crows

after blessing the earth
there for hours

want a word
with me   I know I know—

all this talk of talking
to the dead

and not one
Son your   your I's—

they're still
too dangerously close together

from you   or one
Forgive me

if I've gone
and said too much

the eldest of the hellebores
you planted

livening
just now a little

VIII

Some nights the people made of ash
in the dream I have
yet to name

are led to safety
the tulip and black dove unite
as do the queen

and sun who first condemned them
Whistle says father
when cleaning out the stalls

but never when leading
a lamb to slaughter
This and only this

will I leave you   my
life's law and practice

X

Into the opening only I was thrown
my hat and boots
the valley's now

And like the others
living underground words like
carry meant absence

Covering the eyes
with the right hand
meant *more water* or *I need more time*

And don't get me started on the squall
that hit us or how it winnowed
down the surrounding

trees to mere slivers
the air for days afterward reeking of
    wet straw

Not only are we born dreaming
says father but we
are dreamers and dream both

the two wandering coatless always
the fence nearly

mended the horses
at the far end of the field grazing still

XI

This portion of the canyon floor

How opposed it is to the sun's gaze
yet heather thrives everywhere

Enough to empty the day's sense of
being hour to hour

The future's too

∞

Saying *Open* over and over helps only some

∞

Overstarved for Love—
I wedded the Bottle
as one would

a Nightmare—
vs say—Running—
Oxycontin

∞

Where would the heart be I
ask you if

not for emptiness
Or that silver hook of late December

moon hovering over
the way home

Relax   I said *if*

XII

This business of no road sign
bearing the warning

Another Loss Ahead

∞

This very instant—
what other refuge is there
from what one

could've done
but didn't

aka
Mindfield

Rest anywhere else
and say goodbye to
direct sunlight—

the body's
black tar heroin

XIII

Take the footbridge the first miners raised

Climb down the grassy slope
and you come to a boy standing
before an open grave

Every year the urge to talk to him grows
Wait long enough and the urge turns to smoke

And cast across the smoke the same boy
now a man throwing rocks at the rose
window of Saint Francis Cathedral

Who knew throwing anything
numbs the acts itself

Who knew a crow was the main ingredient
of both world wars and

                that the voice
of the bishop's prized mums could mask
the missteps of mine and father's combined

XIV

Indifferent to falling
he waits along the canyon's north rim
for the sign to descend

His hands no longer sore from clinging

∞

Not once that winter was worry
voiced at the supper table

The boy didn't speak crow then

If he had no whistling
would've been heard when leading
his first lamb to slaughter

Only swells of soft cawing
and between them the brawl
of frozen snow breaking underfoot

XV

The good knife

The one with most of its handle still intact

The best grindstone

A set of old kitchen curtains waiting to become rags

∞

Just because the shelling has stopped doesn't mean the
    ceasefire has begun

Nor the digging of mass grave

After mass grave

After mass grave

∞

This is how you hold the knife

This is where you enter

and this is how you hold the catchbucket

so you don't bruise the blood

says the grandfather

Do these things and

the soul of the ewe will

never refuse to leave her body

XVI

2 am and only one guitar going

∞

Even from way up here
the candle

flames
flicker you closer

and closer
to sleep

∞

None deterred by the frost and snow
the mason worked alone

His tools few
His cart old
His mule nameless as the quarry
three days away on horseback

Seven when hauling a full load

Today when strangers stop and say
How miraculous But why no roof

the old man tells them
*How else might the fallen know they
    are welcome*

XVII

You can sit here for days and never see
the same ghost twice

dancing in the clearing
where the orchard once stood

∞

The third worldwar is coming
Or so says father

And he could be right as the horses won't touch
the apples I stole
and the hangman's great

great granddaughter
isn't at her bedroom window
wondering when the next heartbreak will show

XVIII

My first loveletter from the valley

I can't find it anywhere

Maybe its out roaming
again what used to be the banks of
what used to be the river

And now it's staring
at what it calls a thumbnail moon

I call a flying sickle

∞

Autumn means the trees aren't dying baby   only
     changing

∞

To think we survive the shock
Of going from all that glorious warm darkness

To all that frightening florescent light only
To spend how much of our lives

Gathering and storing
Gathering and storing

Loss after loss until travel by crawling
Becomes our goto artform

XIX

Not nine hours into the invasion
And just look at all these severed wings
Of downed guardian angels

All of these once oblivionwhite feathers

What in me Lord wants to gather and
fashion them all into a pillow

for who else to rest fast upon
and nightly nightmare from

As if wanting itself and wanting alone
never once brought anyone
so much as a grain of suffering

Acknowledgements

Fieldnotes VI, IV, VIII, and X are forthcoming in *Guesthouse*.

About the author

Tommy Archuleta is a native northern New Mexican. He works as
a mental health therapist and substance abuse counselor for the New
Mexico Corrections Department. Most recently his work has appeared
in the *New England Review, Laurel Review, Lily Poetry Review, The
Cortland Review, Guesthouse,* and the *Poem-a-Day* series sponsored by
the Academy of American Poets. His full-length debut collection of
poems, entitled *Susto,* is forthcoming from The Center for Literary
Publishing at Colorado State University as a Mountain/West Poetry
Series title in collaboration with the National Endowment for the Arts.
He lives and writes on the Cochiti Reservation.